EMBRACE

A BIBLICAL STUDY ON JUSTICE AND RACE

DENNIS KANG

Published by White Blackbird Books, an imprint of Storied Publishing

Printed in the United States of America

ISBN-13:978-1-7335921-9-2

Made in the USA.

Cover design by Hwanhee Kang

Edited by Doug Serven

ALSO BY WHITE BLACKBIRD BOOKS

All Are Welcome: Toward a Multi-Everything Church

The Almost Dancer

Birth of Joy: Philippians

Choosing a Church: A Biblical and Practical Guide

Co-Laborers, Co-Heirs: A Family Conversation

Ever Light and Dark: Telling Secrets, Telling the Truth

Everything Is Meaningless? Ecclesiastes

Heal Us Emmanuel: A Call for Racial Reconciliation, Representation, and Unity in the Church

The Organized Pastor: Systems to Care for People Well

Rooted: The Apostles' Creed

A Sometimes Stumbling Life

Urban Hinterlands: Planting the Gospel in Uncool Places

Follow whiteblackbirdbooks.pub for upcoming titles and releases.

EmbRACE is a truly biblical, redemptive, and hopeful vision that God gives us for embracing "the other." The American congregation continues to suffer from segregation, which flies in the face of Jesus' high priestly prayer. The complexities of race within the culture and the church make the issue daunting for any pastor or leader regardless of denomination or theological stripe. The great gift of Kang's work is that he helps us sort through practicality as well as theology, and he offers tangible steps for both congregation and individual. Challenging and prophetic, this is a study that every church needs to go through.

Rick McKinley
Founding Pastor, Imago Dei Community
Author, *Faith for the Moment*

This study provides the Church with an important tool for facilitating conversations of understanding. Dr. Kang presents a useful means for appreciating the importance of racial and ethnic diversity, and he offers a safe and healthy way to engage in and understand the issue.

Derek Chin
Assistant Professor and Pastoral Ministries Dean
Multnomah Seminary

Addressing one of the most sensitive issues of our day, Dennis has provided one of the most helpful small group studies I've seen. *EmbRACE* provides an overview of the core issues, and how they developed in our culture. At the same time, it guides discussion toward the nuanced implications for our everyday lives. I would recommend this study to any Christian.

Chuck Bomar
Pastor, Colossae Church
Author, *Serving Local Schools* and *Better Off Without Jesus*

EmbRACE sets the table for healthy, God-honoring conversations about racial reconciliation in a Christian context. This is a practical, hands-on resource geared to help brothers and sisters across various backgrounds draw closer to God and each other.

Lloyd Kim
Coordinator of Mission to the World, the missions agency of the Presbyterian Church in America

ABOUT THE AUTHOR

Dennis J. Kang (MDiv, Westminster Seminary; DMin Multnomah Seminary) is the Senior Pastor of City Light Church, a culturally and socioeconomically diverse church in downtown Los Angeles. He has ministered in and through divisive and disruptive moments in the city's history over the past twenty years. His doctorate in Missional Leadership focused on racial reconciliation with a desire to bridge divisions within the city.

CONTENTS

INTRODUCTION

Many Christians in America today are waking up to the reality of the deep racial tensions that exist in our country. There is a constant barrage of news protesting police brutality, viral videos showing blatant acts of racism, and a disturbing rise of white supremacists. In spite of these growing concerns, our churches are often missing in action.

In a 1960 "Meet the Press" interview, Dr. Martin Luther King, Jr poignantly noted, "I think it is one of the tragedies of our nation, one of the shameful tragedies, that 11 o'clock on Sunday morning is one of the most segregated hours, if not the most segregated hour in Christian America." Even though this statement was made close to sixty years ago, we can wonder whether we've made any progress in desegregating our own churches or leading the discussion on genuine racial reconciliation.

My own journey toward racial reconciliation began as a church planter in downtown Los Angeles. Though the demographics of downtown was diverse, the church began as a very homogenous group of middle class, Asian Americans. A few years into the church plant, I began to grow restless with the direction of the church.

The culture of our church was ingrown, and it was difficult to break through our cultural barriers. I began to re-envision our ministry as an intentionally cross-cultural ministry that reflects our city. This commitment to diversity led to some fundamental differences that began to change the makeup of our congregation.

As I ministered to people from different backgrounds and classes, my eyes began to open to perspectives I had never encountered.

I remember visiting someone from our church at the Men's Central Jail in downtown. I was alarmed at how the vast majority of incarcerated men were African American, though they represented a much smaller percentage of our city.

On another occasion, I was rattled to receive a frantic call from a faithful member of our church, an international student from Uganda living close to downtown. He had just been held at gunpoint by an officer who was responding to a theft involving a young African American male.

The narrowness of my ministry experience and viewpoints became much more apparent as my congregation diversified, and I took on the responsibility to counsel people from all walks of life in such dire circumstances. I began a journey to not only seek diversity but also genuine reconciliation.

This study was written to help churches address the ever-growing racial tensions within our cities and country. We are on a journey to grapple with difficult topics that confront us today. Many of the topics might be off-putting to some. A few statements from people in your group (if you work through this in a group) might anger, sadden or frustrate you. I pray you'll keep an open mind to the study, to the voices of others in your group, and most importantly to the Spirit who speaks powerfully through the Holy Scriptures.

At the end of each study, you'll see an important section in which we proactively work on our actual, real-life relationships.

The goal of these studies is ultimately to help heal our relationships with our family members, church members, neighbors, friends, coworkers, and those we pass by daily in our city or town. Genuine racial reconciliation doesn't take place in classrooms but in the midst of our daily, ordinary lives.

May God bring his shalom to re-stitch his fractured people to move toward that great multicultural congregation that exists in heaven (Rev. 7:9).

A RACIALLY DIVIDED SOCIETY

On the final evening of Jesus' earthly ministry, Jesus prayed that the church "may all be one" in order that the "world may believe" (Jn. 17:21). This high priestly prayer reflected Jesus' earnest desire for his bride. Yet as we reflect upon the world and church today, race continues to be a dividing line that prevents this prayer from being fully realized.

TEACHING

In their book *Divided by Faith*, Michael Emerson and Christian Smith argue that we live in a racialized society. They write:

> In the post-Civil Rights United States, the racialized society is one in which intermarriage rates are low, residential separation and socioeconomic inequality are the norm, our definitions of personal identity and our choices of intimate associations reveal racial distinctivenss, and where we are never unaware of

the race of a person with whom we interact. In short, and this is its unchanging essence, a racialized society is a society where race matters profoundly for differences in life experiences, life opportunities and social relationships.[1]

Racially Divided Neighborhoods

The 2010 US Census shows us how racially divided our cities and neighborhoods are throughout the country. Below is an example of a racially divided city. Though Los Angeles is one of the most diverse cities in the country, its residents overwhelmingly live in racially homogenous areas.

Figure 1: Racial Map of Los Angeles

The map shows us the distinct living areas of the four major races: White, Latino, Black, and Asian. The most affluent areas on the coast are predominately White. Asians dominate the San Gabriel Valley. Parts of South

Los Angeles are densely populated by African Americans. Latinos make up the vast majority of the center of Los Angeles County.

Where do these divisions come from? Do people simply choose to live in close proximity to people who are like them? Richard Rothstein highlights the role of the federal government in perpetuating racially distinct neighborhoods in his recent book *The Color of Law*.[2] He recounts how the federal government enforced segregation through explicitly segregated public housing. In the late twentieth century, the Federal Housing Administration (FHA) intentionally enforced segregation by creating lending practices that explicitly prohibited African Americans from buying homes in White neighborhoods. Banks would create "red lines" which prevented them from lending to African Americans in those areas. The FHA refused to insure mortgages for African Americans who wanted to move into designated White neighborhoods.

A common practice was for individual property owners to state in their deed a refusal for their home to be sold to any non-Whites. One example of this is found in Daly City, a neighborhood close to San Francisco. In 1950 a covenant of a property in Daly City read, "The real property about described, or any portion thereof, shall never be occupied, used or resided on by any person not of the White or Caucasian race, except in the capacity of a servant or a domestic employed thereon as such by a White owner, tenant or occupant." Even though these racist practices have been overturned by various court rulings, the effects of these laws persist. Currently in Daly City, the African American population is under one percent.

Entertainment

Not only are we divided by our neighborhoods, but also by the kind of entertainment we consume. Take for instance Nielsen's tracking of some of the most popular shows on television. The runaway hit *This is Us* is watched by 88.95 percent of non-African American viewers. On the other extreme, the reality-based show, *Real Housewives of Atlanta* has an audience that is 65.39 percent African American. Some shows, such as *Atlanta,* features an African American cast and attracts an equal amount of White and Black audiences, but they are the exception.

The two biggest genres of music, rap and country, also represent a Black and White divide. Rap artists are predominantly Black and speak to Black America although the music is listened to by a wide racial demographic. Country artists are predominantly White and listened to by a mostly White demographic.

The history of country music has had notable contributions by African Americans musicians. But in the 1920s, the commercial recording industry began to segregate "Black music" (blues, gospel, jazz) for Black people and "White music" (country, hillbilly) exclusively for a White audience. [3]

Churches

Although America is divided by race, one place where we should not expect this is in the Christian church. After all, the Scriptures clearly teach that Jesus has called us to all the nations (Matt. 28:19) and has called his diverse church to unity (Jn. 17:20–23). But when examining the evidence, we see that the church is even more divided than our country at large.

The Pew Research Center released a study in 2015 that examined religious groups in the country according to their racial makeup. The study found that a majority (57 percent) of congregants overall are part of congregations that are predominantly (at least 80 percent) non-Hispanic White. Additionally, 14 percent of Americans who attend services do so at houses of worship with membership that is at least 80 percent Black (including 5 percent who are in congregations that are entirely Black). Another 8 percent attend churches where at least eight in ten churchgoers are Hispanic.[4]

When looking at Christian churches in comparison to Muslims, Jehovah's Witness, or Buddhists, the numbers are striking. The Jehovah Witness congregations, for instance are 36 percent White, 27 percent Black, and 32 percent Latino.

Historically, the racial divide in churches are remnants from slavery, segregation and the refusal of White congregations to fully admit African Americans as members. During the Colonial Era, slaves would often be offered baptism only with a promise that they would not seek their own freedom. One baptism vow reads, "You declare in the presence of God and before this congregation that you do not ask for holy baptism out of any design to free yourself from the Duty and Obedience you owe to your master."[5] Following the Civil War, African Americans left White churches en masse, forming their own churches and denominations. Although the vast majority of churches today openly welcome every race, the remnants of our past remain

As John Perkins writes:

> Something is wrong at the root of American evangelicalism. I believe we have lost the Gospel— God's reconciling power, which is unique to Christianity—and have substituted church growth. We have learned how to reproduce the church without the message.[6]

~

DISCUSSION

Do you agree with the assessment that we live in a racially divided society? Why or why not? If so, what are examples of these divisions in your city?

Is it morally wrong for people to want to associate with people who are like them? When does a preference to be with your own race become problematic?

Do you think these divides are freely chosen or systematically enforced or both? How has the past affected the present?

Why do you think churches have been no better at overcoming racial divides than society as a whole? Do you think the church today is more concerned with numerical growth than genuine reconciliation?

How do you think we can begin to overcome these racial divides?

What are ways the Gospel explores and explodes the racial divides that confront us today?

~

ASSIGNMENT

Each week we'll seek to apply what we learn in our everyday relationships. The goal of EmbRACE is the renewal and reconciliation of our relationships.

The first and primary relationships are in our family.

In 1 Tim. 5:8, the Apostle Paul writes, *"But if anyone does not provide for his relatives, and especially for members of his household, he has denied the faith and is worse than an unbeliever."*

Relational Focus: Family

Marriage (If married)
Ask your spouse how you can pray for him or her this week.
Plan a date night.
Ask your spouse during the date night how you might better serve him or her.

Parents, In-Laws

Call your parent(s) and/or in-laws this week.
Ask how you might pray for them.
Ask if there are any needs or prayer requests with
other family members.

Children

Spend some time with each of your children this week
and pray with them individually.

Relatives

Follow up with any relatives who are in need.

∾

APPLICATIONS

RACE AND RACISM

TEACHING

What does the Bible have to say about race? Are racial features purely a social construct or are they created by God?

In Genesis 10 we see a "Table of Nations" comprised of the descendants of Noah's three sons: Shem, Ham, and Japheth. Already in Genesis 10 we see the development of distinct languages, regions, and cultures. After the description of each of the three lines we read a refrain: *"These are the sons of (Japheth, Ham, Shem), by their clans, their language, their lands, and their nations"* (Gen. 10:5, 20, 31).

A position paper by the Presbyterian Church in America states that racial distinctives are:

> Distinguishable categories; they are not irrelevant. In the church at Antioch there were prophets and teachers: Barnabas, Simeon called Niger, Lucius of

Cyrene, Manaen (who had been brought up with Herod the tetrarch) and Saul. (Acts 13:1)

But they are not defining categories that prohibit unity in the worship, fellowship and mission of the Body of Christ. There is neither Jew nor Greek, slave nor free, male nor female, for you are all one in Christ Jesus. (Gal. 5:28)

And they are categories included in the distinctive and eternal celebration of God's work through the ages. After this I looked and there before me was a great multitude that no one could count, from every nation, tribe, people and language, standing before the throne and in front of the Lamb. They were wearing white robes and were holding palm branches in their hands. (Rev. 7:9)[1]

~

DISCUSSION

Why do you think God created a variety of ethnicities and cultures?

How have you benefited from experiencing other cultures?

How does the diversity of heaven amplify the glory of God?

Race and Division

Read Genesis 11:1–9.

~

QUESTIONS

In Genesis 10 the people are scattered, but in Genesis 11 the people are seemingly united. What temporarily unites the people? Why does this anger God?

Why do you think God curses people by confusing their languages? How is Pentecost (Acts 2) a reversal of this curse?

In Genesis 10 the people are separated physically. In what way are the people separated at the end of Genesis 11? How do we still see this today?

Divisions in the New Testament Church

As we approach the New Testament, the key division is between the Jewish people and the non-Jewish world. In John 4, we meet a Samaritan woman who is shocked that a Jewish man would even address her, *"for Jews have no dealings with Samaritans"* (Jn. 4:9). The ethnic division was so great that it created boundaries relating to speech, touch, and even sharing drinking vessels.

One way we see this hostility is by looking at the temple itself. David Stevens writes:

> The epitome of the growing hostility was seen in the temple, constructed by Herod the Great. The temple itself was made up of three courts: the Court of the Priests, the Court of Israel, and the Court of Women. Beyond this, however, was the Court of the Gentiles. To get to this court, one had to descend five steps from the temple itself to the wall. Then on the other side of the wall, one would descend fourteen more steps to another wall. Beyond that was the Court of the Gentiles. From here, Gentiles, could look up and see the temple but were not allowed to approach it.

They were separated by a one and a half meter stone barricade. Along this barricade were various notices that read in Greek and Latin: "trespassers will be executed."[2]

Jesus breaks these barriers by welcoming in the Samaritan (John 4) and the Canaanite woman (Matt. 15). The gospel of Matthew ends with Jesus' stirring commission to *"go and make disciples of all nations"* (Matt. 28:19). But as the Gospel makes progress through the Gentile world, a clear division emerges between Jewish and Gentile (non-Jewish) believers. In Galatians 2, the Apostle Paul recounts how Peter hypocritically withdrew from eating with Gentiles and wasn't living in *"step with the truth of the gospel"* (Gal. 2:14). Although Jesus has called us to live in unity, the church was constantly plagued by ethnic division.

∽

DISCUSSION

How is race and culture fundamental to the unfolding of the story of the Gospel?

What are ways the Church continues to be separated by various subgroups?

In the book of Acts, Paul says that when we separate ourselves from other races we are living in contradiction to the Gospel. How is racism a Gospel issue?

Racism and the Gospel

In a pastoral letter adopted by the Presbyterian Church in America we see one definition of racism:

Racism is any want of conformity to or transgression

of the Bible's approach to race; it is any belief or act that is contrary to God's bringing His redeeming shalom to the races. More specifically, racism is the sinful action or attitude of elevating (idolizing) the superiority of one's race over another in such a way as to cause a lack of love for one another as Christ loved, to hate others in our hearts and actions, and/or to act toward a race in an oppressive, unjust or indifferent manner. Racism, like any other sin, is expressed in thoughts and actions by an individual. But as individuals act together, racism can be expressed by a group or institution.[3]

In his book *The Color Line*, John Franklin explains:

There is nothing inherently wrong with being aware of color as long as it is seen as making distinctions in a pleasant, superficial, and unimportant manner. It is only when character is attached to color, when ability is measured by color, when privilege is tied to color, and a whole galaxy of factors that spell the difference between success and failure in our society are tied to color—it is only when such considerations are attached to color that it becomes a deadly, dreadful, denigrating factor among us all.[4]

The Call

Racism isn't just a contemporary issue but is deeply rooted in the Bible, in our history, and ultimately in all of our hearts. In our culture racism is often seen as "the" great sin. Nobody wants to admit it, but most people recognize that it's everywhere. The Bible says that our hearts are *"deceitful above all things and desperately wicked"* (Jer. 17:9). In contrast to this earthly world, the first calling of a Christian is repentance (Matt. 3:2). What if Christians took the lead by first confessing the racism in their own hearts? What if we were bold to confess our own prejudices, our own privileges, and our own indifferences to people of other races? How would the Christian witness change if we proactively tried to cross barriers and form cross-cultural relationships?

Do you think we have elements of racism in our own hearts? Where do you think is a safe place to confess sins of racism?

What are some ways you can step out of your cultural comfort zone with the Gospel?

What are some places you can go to experience and
learn about other cultures in your city?

What is a more difficult for you: befriending someone
of a different race or a befriending someone of
different socioeconomic class? How can you work
toward overcoming these barriers?

~

ASSIGNMENT

Jesus repeatedly summarized the greatest commandment by saying:

> *The most important is, 'Hear, O Israel: The Lord our God, the Lord is one. And you shall love the Lord your God with all your heart and with all your soul and with all your mind and with all your strength.' The second is this: 'You shall love your neighbor as yourself.' There is no other commandment greater than these.* (Mark 12:29–31)

In the Parable of the Good Samaritan, Jesus enlarges the idea of neighbor to include anyone in need (Luke 10:25–37).

Relationship Focus: Neighbors

Brainstorm ways you can be a better neighbor.

This week knock on the door of your physical neighbor and invite him or her over for a meal.

Pray for your neighbor this week.

APPLICATIONS

CHRIST THE RECONCILER

TEACHING

There is a tendency to see Jesus' salvation as merely a personal experience, but the biblical picture is to see salvation from the broader perspective of God reconciling all things to himself (2 Cor. 5:18). Jesus' ministry is a ministry of making enemies into friends. He reconciles the world to himself and also calls us into a ministry of reconciliation.

In the previous lesson, we explored how there were deep rifts between Jews and Samaritans. But Jesus consistently ministered to Samaritans and opened his kingdom to those outside of Israel. Jesus crossed barriers to offer living water to a Samaritan woman (John 4). A Samaritan is also a hero in the story of what it means to love our neighbors (Luke 10:33). In the story of ten lepers, the single man who returns is a Samaritan (Luke 17:16). In Matthew 15:28, a Canaanite woman is exalted as a woman of great faith because of her persistence.

In the gospel of John, Jesus prays his high priestly prayer the night he was betrayed. He prays, *"I do not ask for these only, but also for those who will believe in me through their word, that they may all be one, just as you, Father, are in me, and I in you, that they also may be in us, so that the world may believe that you have sent me"* (John 17:20–21). Jesus' prayer is not just for Jewish believers but for all those who believe. He prays that the universal church would be united as a collective witness to the world. The capstone to Jesus' ministry is found after his resurrection in the Great Commission in Matthew 28:16–20. Here we see an explicit call for Jesus' disciples to go to all the nations. We see the beginning of God's promise that in Abraham all nations will be blessed (Gen. 12:3). God will begin to bring his fractured humanity together in one united church.

∽

DISCUSSION

In what sense are all non-Jewish Christians outsiders or minorities? How does Jesus include us in his promise and kingdom?

Do you regularly pray like Jesus that there would be greater unity in Christ's church? What are ways you can more regularly incorporate these prayers in your life, family, and church?

Do you think a racially diverse church that is truly united would be the greatest witness to the world? What would that look like? How would that be a prophetic witness to our culture?

Ephesians 2:11–22

Therefore remember that at one time you Gentiles in the flesh, called "the uncircumcision" by what is called the circumcision, which is made in the flesh by hands— remember that you were at that time separated from Christ, alienated from the commonwealth of Israel and strangers to the covenants of promise, having no hope and without God in the world. But now in Christ Jesus you who once were far off have been brought near by the blood of Christ. For he himself is our peace, who has made us both one and has broken down in his flesh the dividing wall of hostility by abolishing the law of commandments expressed in ordinances, that he might create in himself one new man in place of the two, so making peace, and might reconcile us both to God in one body through the cross, thereby killing the hostility. And he came and preached peace to you who were far off and peace to those who were near. For through him we both have access in one Spirit to the Father. So then you are no longer strangers and aliens, but you are fellow citizens with the saints and members of the household of God, built on the foundation of the apostles and prophets,

Christ Jesus himself being the cornerstone, in whom the whole structure, being joined together, grows into a holy temple in the Lord. In him you also are being built together into a dwelling place for God by the Spirit.

When Jesus abolished "the law of commandments," (vs. 15) He didn't abolish the moral law but civil laws, including diet and dress, pertaining to the nation of Israel. What would have happened if non-Jewish people were forced to adopt Jewish culture in order to become a believer? How does Christianity adapt to any culture now? In what ways do we tend to exalt certain cultural expressions of Christianity?

What are the three clauses that show the equality of Jewish and non-Jewish believers? Which of these clauses do you need to remember when you feel far apart from another Christian from a different background?

Ephesians 3:1–10

For this reason I, Paul, a prisoner of Christ Jesus on behalf of you Gentiles—assuming that you have heard of the stewardship of God's grace that was given to me for you, how the mystery was made known to me by revelation, as I have written briefly. When you read this, you can perceive my insight into the mystery of Christ, which was not made known to the sons of men in other generations as it has now been revealed to his holy apostles and prophets by the Spirit. This mystery is that the Gentiles are fellow heirs, members of the same body, and partakers of the promise in Christ Jesus through the gospel.

Of this gospel I was made a minister according to the gift of God's grace, which was given me by the working of his power. To me, though I am the very least of all the saints, this grace was given, to preach to the Gentiles the unsearchable riches of Christ, and to bring to light for everyone what is the plan of the mystery hidden for ages in God, who created all things, 10 so that through the church the manifold wisdom of God might now be made known to the rulers and authorities in the heavenly places.

What is the "mystery of Christ" that Paul refers to in verses 3 and 4? How do we see hints of this mystery in Genesis 12:1–3 with God's promise to Abraham?

Where does God show the world his manifold wisdom? (3: 10). How does a multicultural church highlight the multifaceted wisdom of God?

What Is Reconciliation?

Reconciliation presupposes at least two hostile parties. In Ephesians, we see that we were *"dead in our trespasses"* (Eph. 2:1) and *"children of wrath"* (Eph. 2:3). Jesus reconciles former enemies through the cross. It is a costly reconciliation which satisfies God's justice and brings peace. Reconciliation not only means forgiveness, but also a restoration of relationship. Jesus not only forgives us, but he also calls us his friends (Jn. 15:15) and adopts us into his family (1 Jn. 3:1). The cross not only reconciles us to God, but also reconciles formerly hostile parties and brings peace.

How God reconciles us to himself is a helpful paradigm to see how we can be reconciled to other believers. First, in order to be reconciled to God, we must confess our sins openly (Acts 2:38). Reconciliation between people also involves a genuine confession of our wrongs that avoid minimizing or excusing. Second, reconciliation requires forgiveness. As Christ has generously forgiven us, we are to extend that same forgiveness to each other (Col. 3:13). Third, reconciliation leads to a desire to make things right. At the cross, Jesus satisfies the wrath of God by bringing justice (Matt. 27:46). Zacchaeus, a tax collector, models this when he says, *"Behold, Lord, the half of my goods I give to the poor. And if I have defrauded anyone of anything, I restore it fourfold"* (Lk. 19:8). Zacchaeus doesn't merely ask defrauded parties for forgiveness, he pledges to make them financially whole. Ultimately reconciliation is a process that brings a restored relationship.

What is the difference between forgiveness and reconciliation?

Why does reconciliation have to begin with truth? Have you ever had someone try to restore their relationship with you without admitting any fault? How did that make you feel?

What is the difference between forgiveness and reconciliation?

Can there be reconciliation without any kind of restoration of things lost? Can forgiveness overcome this injustice?

Do you think it is possible not only for individuals to be reconciled but also groups of people who are hostile to each other? What would this require?

Do you think it is possible not only for groups to be reconciled? What would this require?

~

ASSIGNMENT

Relationship Focus: Enemies

Think about people in your family, church, workplace, or community that you have had conflicts with.

How do you typically handle conflict?

Consider this quote from Ken Sande's book, *The Peacemaker*:

Forgiveness may be described as a decision to make four promises:

"I will not think about this incident."

"I will not bring up this incident again or use it against you."

"I will not talk to others about this incident."

"I will not allow this incident to stand between us or hinder our personal relationship."

By making and keeping these promises, you tear down the walls that stand between you and your offender. You promise not to dwell on or brood over the problem, nor to punish by holding the person at a distance. You clear the way for your relationship to develop unhindered by memories of past wrongs. This is exactly what God does for us, and it is what he commands us to do for others."[1]

Write down the names of one or two people with whom you need to seek reconciliation.

Pray that you will be able to make the four promises of forgiveness.

If the offending party is open to it, meet with him or her and seek genuine reconciliation.

APPLICATIONS

THE MULTI-ETHNIC CHURCH

TEACHING

There is a tendency to see Jesus' salvation as merely a personal experience. But the fuller biblical picture shows something much larger. Jesus opens the flood-gates with his commandment to *"make disciples of all nations"* (Matt. 28:19). Jesus follows this up in Acts with a similar command to bring the Good News to *"Jerusalem, Judea, and Samaria, and the ends of the earth"* (Acts 1:8). The book of Acts records the progress of the Gospel through different nations, cultures, and people groups. The early church reflected this extraordinary diversity.

The leadership at the church of Antioch gives us a glimpse of this diversity. Author David Stevens writes:

> It is not surprising, then, that the leadership of the church at Antioch was just as diverse as its surrounding community. Luke writes in Acts 13:1, *"In the church at Antioch there were prophets and teachers:*

Barnabas, Simeon called Niger, Lucius of Cyrene, Manaen (who had been brought up with Herod the tetrarch) and Saul." The prophet/teacher Simeon has the Latin surname of Niger, which means "black." Niger was a country located in the sub-Saharan West Africa, as it is today. Luke has already shown how the Gospel went to an Ethiopian eunuch, a black. Now a black African is part of the leadership team of this thriving community.[1]

This diverse leadership of seven continues to break new ground to bring the Gospel to diverse and unreached groups. The most striking example of this is in Acts 8 when Philip shares the Gospel first to Samaritans and then to an Ethiopian eunuch. This Ethiopian eunuch represents the first explicit example of a Gentile coming to faith. This eunuch was a royal messenger of the court, traveling an important route at the behest of *"Candace, queen of the Ethiopians"* (Acts 8:27). Craig Keener notes the significance of this title:

The Greek title "Ethiopia" technically included all of Africa south of Egypt, but the Candace's title has convinced nearly all scholars that the Nubian kingdom of Meroe is specifically in view here…. Meroe's Nubia was what was then a black African kingdom between Aswan and Khartoum, the two leading cities of which were Meroe and Napata; it had endured since around 760 BCE and since at least the early third century BCE had ruled from its capital in Meroe.[2]

One of the first times we meet a Black man in the New Testament we find that he is not impoverished, but a royal messenger of a great African kingdom. One wonders how someone like Philip would view this man. Would he be noticed for his skin color as many would undoubtedly today? Keener answers:

> Most obviously, Luke's audience would assume that the Ethiopian was black. Although this feature might seem irrelevant to the story for some modern readers, it was a primary element of most Mediterranean conceptions of Ethiopians…. "Black" complexion was the most common defining feature of Ethiopians in ancient Mediterranean literature. Diaspora Jewish texts and later rabbis both work from the assumption that "Ethiopians" are "black." So pervasive was the characteristics that people used Ethiopians as a symbol of something black.[3]

One of the most important aspects of this encounter was that Philip was encountering a Black man. Furthermore, this man is a eunuch, which would have excluded him from the assembly of the congregation (Exod. 23:1). But the Ethiopian official overcomes all of these barriers with his hunger to learn the Scriptures and eventually his desire to be immediately baptized (Acts 8:37). The Gospel is crossing every conceivable barrier including race and culture. God is bringing former outsiders inside the kingdom.

Not only was the early church ethnically diverse, but it also brought together different classes of people. In 1 Peter 2, Peter addresses slaves and freemen. In James 2, the apostle prohibits favoring the wealthy over the poor when they enter into worship. The church was not only diverse ethnically but also socioeconomically.

~

DISCUSSION

What makes diverse leadership in the church important?

Do you think churches today are more welcoming of diverse races than they are of the poor?

Revelation 7:9–12

After this I looked, and behold, a great multitude that no one could number, from every nation, from all tribes and peoples and languages, standing before the throne and before the Lamb, clothed in white robes, with palm branches in their hands, and crying out with a loud voice, "Salvation belongs to our God who sits on the throne, and to the Lamb!" And all the angels were standing around the throne and around the elders and the four living creatures, and they fell on their faces before the throne and worshiped God, saying, "Amen! Blessing and glory and wisdom and thanksgiving and honor and power and might be to our God forever and ever! Amen."

What kind of diversity is seen in this great assembly in heaven?

Diversity is often seen as part of a liberal agenda. How is diversity God's dream? How do we see this dream unfolding from Genesis to Revelation?

Do you think the Church on earth should reflect the diverse assembly in heaven? Why or why not?

The Multi-Ethnic Church

Martin Luther King Jr. famously said that the most divided hour in America is eleven o'clock on Sunday morning. In a previous lesson we looked at research that indicates that a majority of congregations (57 percent) belong to a congregation that is predominately non-Hispanic White. In contrast, we see the great multi-ethnic assembly of heaven. Jesus taught us to pray, *"Your kingdom come, your will be done, on earth as it is in heaven"* (Matt. 6:10). We also see the diverse leadership in early churches like in Antioch. So the question remains, can our church begin to reflect more of this divine assembly? What kind of witness would a unified multi-ethnic church be in our culture of racial hostility?

What are the racial demographics of your area? Does your church reflect your local neighborhood?

What are the barriers that keep your church from being diverse if it is not?

Often churches want minorities to be a part of the church without seeking to accommodate them or inviting them into positions of influence. How can your church avoid the problem of seeking "token minorities?"

Do you think your church has a harder time reaching different classes of people or different races of people?

How does the heavenly assembly give you hope that the Gospel can and will break through every human barrier?

∽

ASSIGNMENT

Relationship Focus: Church Members

Every church has some aspects of diversity (age, race, class).

Choose a person that is significantly different than you.

Plan a time for you to meet with him or her.

Ask that person about his or her childhood and stories that shaped his or her identity.

Ask how race and upbringing played a role in his or her spiritual journey.

Close in prayer.

∾

APPLICATIONS

CULTURAL INTELLIGENCE

TEACHING

When missionaries fly thousands of miles overseas to a foreign country, one of the first things they must do is become a student of the new culture. They have to learn the language, customs, and values of that culture in order to share the Good News in a meaningful way. Missionaries understand that their entire mindset must change as they try to look at the world through the eyes of others. But should this mindset be exclusive to overseas missionaries? The United States is increasingly becoming a diverse sea of cultures. According to the Census Bureau, "more than half of the nation's children are expected to be part of a minority race or ethnic group" by 2020.[1] If we want to effectively minister to our changing neighborhoods, we need to have cultural intelligence.

What Is Culture?

"The sum total of ways of living built up by a group of human beings, which is transmitted from one generation to another."
Random House, *American College Dictionary*

"Culture is all of these things: paintings (whether finger paintings or the Sistine chapels), omelets, chairs, snow angels. It is what human beings make of the world. It always bears the stamp of our creativity, our God-given desire to make something more than we were given."
Andy Crouch, *Culture Making*

"It is helpful to look at culture in two parts: external and internal. External culture is the conscious part of culture. It is the part that we can see, taste, and hear. It consists of acknowledged beliefs and values. It is explicitly learned and can be easily changed. However, this constitutes only a small part of our culture. The major part is the internal part, which consists of the unconscious beliefs, thought patterns, values, and myths that affect everything we do and see. It is implicitly learned and is very hard to change."
Eric Law, *The Wolf Shall Dwell with the Lamb*

Christ and Culture

A common debate amongst Christians is what posture we should take toward culture. David Bosch in his seminal work, *Transforming Missions*, summarizes two principles:

On the one hand there is the "indigenizing" principle, which affirms that the Gospel is at home in every culture and every culture is at home with the Gospel.

But then there is the "pilgrim" principle, which warns us that the Gospel will put us out of step with society for that society never existed, in East or West, ancient time or modern, which could absorb the word of Christ painlessly into its system.[2]

~

DISCUSSION

Much of our own culture is unconscious to us. Name some "artifacts" of culture in the room where you are now.

Do you think believers in church are too engulfed by the culture or too separated from the culture? What do you think is the right balance?

1 Corinthians 9:19–23

For though I am free from all, I have made myself a servant to all, that I might win more of them. To the Jews I became as a Jew, in order to win Jews. To those under the law I became as one under the law (though not being myself under the law) that I might win those under the law. To those outside the law I became as one outside the law (not being outside the law of God but under the law of Christ) that I might win those outside the law. To the weak I became weak, that I might win the weak. I have become all things to all people, that by all means I might save some. I do it all for the sake of the gospel, that I may share with them in its blessings.

How did Paul accommodate the different cultures he engaged? What was his motivation to make these changes?

How difficult do you think it was for Paul to make these cultural accommodations? What kind of lifestyle changes would he have to make? What do you think he had to do before he made them? Do you think there were some accommodations he couldn't make?

Exploring Cultural Orientations

In his book *Cultural Intelligence,* Soong-Chan Rah lists different types of cultural orientations.

Review and discuss these different paradigms:

Individual vs. Group Orientation

Individual / Group
Takes individual initiative / Acts cooperatively
Makes decisions individually / Makes decisions as a
group
Nonconformist / Conforms to social norms
Puts individuals before group / Puts the group before
individuals

Guilt vs. Shame

Guilt / Shame
Responsible for individual sin / Responsible for
corporate sin
A result of individual action / A result of identity
You made a mistake / You are a mistake
Absolved by confession / Absolved by a change in
status

Equality vs. Hierarchy

Equality / Hierarchy
Self-directed / Directions from above
Individual initiative / Leader controlled
Flexible roles and expectations / Firm roles and
expectations
Freedom to challenge / Does not challenge authority
Offers own opinion / Respects status of leaders

Direct vs. Indirect

Direct / Indirect
Focus is on what, not how something is said / Focus is
on how something is said
Engages in conflict / Avoids conflict
Short, direct questions / Importance of being friendly
Focus on information / Focus on feeling

Express opinions in a frank manner / Express opinions diplomatically

Task vs. Relationship
Task / Relationship
Focus is on keeping good time / Focus is on building relationships
Goal: provide accurate information / Goal: create a feel-good atmosphere
Define people by what they do / Define people by who they know
Tends toward logic orientation / Tends toward feeling orientation

CASE STUDIES

Please think about and discuss these various scenarios.

Scenario 1

An older African American woman sits by herself in the sanctuary. Her frustration is difficult to put into words. She has been attending her church for over two years. She is one of a handful of African Americans at the church who were attracted to a church committed to multiracial ministry and to serving the needs of her neighborhood. But over the past two years, she has become increasingly frustrated with how little the worship service addressed her spiritual needs. Her fellow church members seem to be more preoccupied with making sure the worship service ends on time than with how the Spirit is moving during the service.

They seem to have a completely different set of expectations about worship. She sits silently as the worship service progresses along without her genuine participation.[3]

Questions
Is the church leadership to blame for being oblivious to this woman's needs?

Can worship services in predominately White contexts become overly intellectual and rigid?

How can both parties move toward a solution?

Is this problem an issue of biblical principle or cultural preferences? Can these issues be separated?

Scenario 2

A young Asian American man glances around the circle of church board members seated around the conference table. He is the only non-White member of the church board. Everyone seems to be talking all at once and seems to know when to speak up and interject their opinions. The young man is listening patiently to all the opinions being expressed but doesn't know when he should participate/jump in. He waits for someone to ask for his opinion, but no one invites him into the conversation. The conversation centers on the topic of leadership diversity at the church, yet the meeting has focused exclusively on the perspective of the dominant group. Why is he even at this meeting if he's not being invited into the discussion?[4]

Questions
Is the Asian American to blame for simply not speaking up?

Should the dominant group understand the power dynamics of the situation? What can the dominant group do to help the situation?

What are the responsibilities in each position?

Scenario 3

A young Latina mother watches anxiously as her five-year-old son bounces out of the sanctuary. He joins the flow of children leaving the adult worship service to attend the children's church.

She doesn't quite understand why the children are being asked to leave the service. She recognizes that there is some cultural value at work, but it escapes her.

She doesn't understand the need to take the children out for a separate service. It seems like a devaluing of the children and their place in the family. She wonders if her church holds the same values as her family.[5]

Questions
What priorities does this young woman have in worship? Are these biblical priorities?

Are this woman's priorities influenced by her culture or by Scripture?

What do you think is a way to balance both priorities?

~

ASSIGNMENT

Relationship Focus: Coworkers

For many of us, our waking hours are spent in the workplace. The workplace can be a place where people work together to bless the city. It can be a pressurized place of abusive relationships.

How would you describe the culture of your workplace?

Are some of your coworkers friends ,or are they
simply people you work with?

How would you describe your ideal relationships with
people in your workplace?

Write a note to one of your coworkers appreciating
him or her.

Take one of your coworkers out to lunch.

Ask a coworker about his or her story, journey, and
future goals.

APPLICATIONS

THE CALL TO JUSTICE

TEACHING

The Bible not only speaks to us about mercy but also about the call to seek justice. Mercy means giving people something they don't deserve. Justice by contrast means giving people what they rightfully deserve. Seeking justice is something that God requires for all of his people. Consider these verses:

> *He has told you, O man, what is good; and what does the LORD require of you, but to do justice, and to love kindness, and to walk humbly with your God.* (Micah 6:8)

> *Open your mouth for the mute, for the rights of the destitute. Open your mouth, judge righteously, defend the rights of the poor and needy.* (Proverbs 31:8–9)

> *Learn to do good; seek justice, correct oppression; bring justice to the fatherless, plead the widow's cause.* (Isaiah 1:17)

The Old Testament word for justice is *mishpat*. This word occurs more than two hundred times in the Old Testament. Tim Keller explains, "Its most basic meaning is to treat people equitably."[1] So Leviticus 24:22 warns Israel to "have the same *mishpat* for the foreigner as the native." *Mishpat* means acquitting or punishing every person on the merits of the case, regardless of race or social status. Anyone who does the same wrong should be given the same penalty. It also means giving people their rights. Deuteronomy 18 directs that the priests of the tabernacle should be supported by a certain percentage of the people's income. This support is described as "the priests' *mishpat*," their due or their right. So we read, *"Defend the rights of the poor and needy"* (Prov. 31:9). The Bible focuses the call to seek justice for the most vulnerable classes of people, the widow, immigrant, orphan, and poor.

Amos 5:10-24

They hate him who reproves in the gate, and they abhor him who speaks the truth. Therefore because you trample on the poor and you exact taxes of grain from him, you have built houses of hewn stone, but you shall not dwell in them; you have planted pleasant vineyards, but you shall not drink their wine. For I know how many are your transgressions and how great are your sins—you who afflict the righteous, who take a bribe, and turn aside the needy in the gate. Therefore he who is prudent will keep silent in such a time, for it is an evil time. Seek good, and not evil, that you may live; and so the LORD, the God of hosts, will be with you, as you have said. Hate evil, and love good, and establish justice in the gate; it may be that the LORD, the God of hosts, will be gracious to the remnant of Joseph. Therefore thus says the LORD, the God of hosts, the Lord: "In all the squares there shall be wailing, and in all the streets they shall say, 'Alas! Alas!' They shall call the farmers to mourning and to wailing those who are skilled in lamentation, and in all vineyards there shall be wailing, for I will pass through your midst," says the LORD.

Woe to you who desire the day of the LORD! Why would you have the day of the LORD? It is darkness, and not light, as if a man fled from a lion, and a bear met him, or went into the house and leaned his hand against the wall, and a serpent bit him. Is not the day of the LORD darkness, and not light, and gloom with no brightness in it? I hate, I despise your feasts, and I take no delight in your solemn assemblies. Even though you offer me your burnt offerings and grain offerings, I will not accept them; and the peace offerings of your fattened animals, I will not look upon them. Take away from me the noise of your songs; to the melody of your harps I will not listen. But let justice roll down like waters, and righteousness like an ever-flowing stream.

∾

DISCUSSION

What kinds of injustices are God's people guilty of committing in Amos?

trample on the poor by taxing
take bribes
afflict the righteous
turn aside the needy

Are the sins committed only sins of commission, or are they also sins of omission? (Amos 5:13). Note: Sins of commission are sins that we actively commit. Sins of omissions involve a failure to act righteously in situations that warrant righteous actions.

They are definitely both

Omission - learn and the body

Why are religious activities empty without justice?

Justice - giving people what they rightfully deserve

If you don't treat all people the same in religious activities then they do not please God

What are some forms of injustice today in your city? Think about the four classes of people that are most frequently mentioned in the Bible (widow, immigrant, orphan, and poor).

City of Northville - Women are not as respected

Price of housing in Northville keeps people out

Do you think most Christians are more guilty of sins of commission or omission when it comes to justice?

I would say sins of omission. We aren't blatantly doing the wrong thing but we are not standing up for others

The Color of Law

Historically, African Americans in the United States have been dehumanized by the law and society. From the transatlantic slave trade, to constitutionally being counted as three-fifths of a whole person to segregation, the plight of the African American has been marked by injustice. Many of these practices have been amended and repealed, but the question remains after all these centuries of injustice and stigmatization. Is the African American really free? Consider this graph:

The Historic Dehumanization of Black People in America

Figure 3: The Historic Dehumanization of Black People in America

Although the era of slavery and segregation has ended,

the remnants of this era still exist. Here are a few ways we can see this.

Housing Richard Rothstein in his book, *The Color of Law*, summarizes the ways the federal government explicitly and implicitly segregated housing, creating an environment where African Americans were by law prohibited from owning homes in White-majority areas. Although the laws have changed, generations of African Americans have been stripped of their ability to have equity in their houses and to pass their homes to the next generation. Today according to the US Census Bureau the home ownership rates in 2017 are 71.8 percent for Whites, 56.8 percent for Asians and 42.7 percent for African Americans.[2]

Education Our public school educational system is tied to real estate and home ownership. The best public schools are almost always found in the most affluent neighborhoods. Wealthier people have access to better schooling, tutors, and out-of-school educational centers to help them with standardized tests. Many liberals blame the government, many conservatives blame the family, but very few people blame the children themselves.

Policing The tragic deaths of Tamir Rice, Michael Brown, Eric Garner, Alton Sterling, and Philando Castile has sparked outrage among many communities over the issue of abusive policing in minority communities. Many African Americans feel they are harassed because of their skin color. This outrage has led to movements like Black Lives Matters. Jemar Tisby, writing for the Reformed African American Network, writes:

> As it was in the past so it is today—the movement for equal justice demands a response from Christians. While not all believers will agree whether they can or should get involved in these contemporary justice movements, no one can avoid taking a position. Either believers line up on the side of reform that will lead to greater human flourishing or they will stand alongside the status quo. Public justice does not require a uniform response from people of faith, but it does require a response.[3]

Mass Incarceration In her book, *The New Jim Crow*, Michelle Alexander chronicles the systemic way African American men have been unfairly targeted by law enforcement and the judicial system. The War on Drugs started at a time when illegal drugs were on the decline. Yet in less than thirty years, the US penal population exploded from 300,000 to more than two million, with drug convictions accounting for the majority of the increase. Even though people of all races use and sell illegal drugs at remarkably similar rates, in some states Black men have been admitted to prison on drug charges at rates twenty to fifty times greater than those of White men. One in three young African American men will serve time in prison if current trends continue, and in some cities more than half of all young adult Black men are currently under correctional control—in prison or jail, on probation or parole.[4]

~

DISCUSSION

Which of these areas do you feel like is the most egregious area of injustice in America?

Hard to choose but Education is
so critical to get out of poverty
Policing policies are very bad as well

Which of these areas would you dispute the notion of injustice?

What are some ways individuals can be involved in "reform that will lead to greater human flourishing"?

Innovate tutoring
protest - join movements
VOTE

~

ASSIGNMENT

Relationship Focus: The Jericho Road

In the story of the Good Samaritan, Jesus defines our neighbor as anyone in need (Luke 10:25–37). In this story, two religious figures see the need and "passed on the other side." Who are people in our path that we have passed by?

Consider this quote from Tim Keller's book, *Generous Justice*:

> We instinctively tend to limit for whom we exert ourselves. We do it for people like us, and for people whom we like. Jesus will have none of that. By depicting a Samaritan helping a Jew, Jesus could not have found a more forceful way to say that anyone at all in need—regardless of race, politics, class, and religion—is your neighbor. Not everyone is your brother or sister in faith, but everyone is your neighbor, and you must love your neighbor.[5]

Who are some people in our literal paths that we know are in need? Consider people in your extended family, co-workers, friends, homeless.

Keep your eyes and ears this week for people in need you might normally miss.

Meet a concrete need for one specific person.

~

APPLICATIONS

Alyssa Thomas

154 Rapor Ridge Rd
Austinville, VA
24312

PRIVILEGE AND GRACE

TEACHING

The Gospel gives us the Good News that though we were once outsiders alienated from God, we've been brought in by the blood of Christ (Eph. 2:13). Salvation is God's free gift to those who were by nature children of wrath (Eph. 2:3). Ultimately Christians are privileged people who have been given heaven's greatest blessings through no effort of our own. 1 Peter 2:9–10 tells us:

> *You are a chosen race, a royal priesthood, a holy nation, a people for his own possession, that you may proclaim the excellencies of him who called you out of the darkness into his marvelous light. Once you were not a people, but now you are God's people, once you had not received mercy, but now you have received mercy.*

Peter contrasts our natural condition with the

lavish gift of our new standing as God's prized possession. Understanding our privilege in Christ should naturally humble us. If we by no merit of our own have come to Christ, we are no longer able to look down on anybody else. At God's table the prostitute and king can dine as equals. This privilege was not given to us to hoard but was given so that we can *"proclaim the excellencies of him who called us out of the darkness."* We were given these unmerited favors so that we could extend them to the nations (Matt. 28:19). Similarly, most people have been given various earthly privileges. These can be things like good health, a loving and safe home, access to great schools and an environment where we are not discriminated against based on our skin color, gender or age. We should not be ashamed of any privileges, but we should acknowledge them and also seek to leverage our blessings for the benefit of others who are without them.

A Story

In the book *Heal Us, Emmanuel*, Mark Peach, a pastor of City Presbyterian in Salt Lake City, shares his story:

> In July 2015 when I saw the video of Sandra Bland, a Black woman, being forced from her car by a White police officer during a routine traffic stop, I was shaken. I was further disturbed to know that she died in a Texas jail cell three days after the arrest. I wondered who Sandra had influenced in her life. I wondered who she would never have the chance to influence. In a system where White culture is at the center and all other cultures are pushed to the

periphery, being a White male has allowed me to isolate myself from racial injustice that is a part of American culture and of many people's experience. As a White person, I am much more prone to embrace the false reality that I have what I have because I worked hard for it. I also am prone to believe that, in general, those in authority treat people equally across the board. This is simply not true.[1]

~

DISCUSSION

Do you think of the word "privilege" as a positive or negative one? What weight does this word hold?

What are some privileges that men have but that women don't have? List them below:

Exploring Privilege

In Peggy McIntosh's work, *White Privilege: Unpacking the Invisible Knapsack,* she speaks about the "invisible, weightless knapsack of special provisions" that many of us carry. McIntosh arrived at this list after rejecting the idea that as a White woman she had any privilege. Then she reconsidered and listed a series of statements that apply to her but not to people of other races. This is her list:

1. I can if I wish arrange to be in the company of people of my race most of the time.
2. If I should need to move, I can be pretty sure of renting or purchasing housing in an area I can afford and in which I would want to live.
3. I can be pretty sure that my neighbors in such a location will be neutral or pleasant to me.
4. I can go shopping alone most of the time, pretty well assured that I will not be followed or harassed.
5. I can turn on the television or open the front

page of the paper and see people of my race widely represented.

6. When I am told about our national heritage or about "civilization," I am shown that people of my color made it what it is.

7. I can be sure that my children will be given curricular materials that testify to the existence of their race.

8. If I want to, I can be pretty sure of finding a publisher for this piece on White privilege.

9. I can go into a music shop and count on finding the music of my race represented, into a supermarket and find the staple foods that fit with my cultural traditions, into a hairdresser's shop and find someone who can cut my hair.

10. Whether I use checks, credit cards, or cash, I can count on my skin color not to work against the appearance of financial reliability.

11. I can arrange to protect my children most of the time from people who might not like them.

12. I can swear, dress in second-hand clothes, or not answer letters, without having people attribute these choices to the bad morals, the poverty, or the illiteracy of my race.

13. I can speak in public to a powerful male group without putting my race on trial.

14. I can do well in a challenging situation without being called a credit to my race.

15. I am never asked to speak for all the people of my racial group.

16. I can remain oblivious of the language and customs of persons of color who constitute the world's majority without feeling in my culture any penalty for such oblivion.

17. I can criticize our government and talk about how much I fear its policies and behavior without being seen as a cultural outsider.

18. I can be pretty sure that if I ask to talk to "the person in charge," I will be facing a person of my race.

19. If a traffic cop pulls me over or if the IRS audits my tax return, I can be sure I haven't been singled out because of my race.

20. I can easily buy posters, postcards, picture books, greeting cards, dolls, toys, and children's magazines featuring people of my race.

21. I can go home from most meetings of organizations I belong to feeling somewhat tied in, rather than isolated, out-of-place, outnumbered, unheard, held at a distance, or feared.

22. I can take a job with an affirmative action employer without having co-workers on the job suspect that I got the job because of race.

23. I can choose public accommodations without fearing that people of my race cannot get in or will be mistreated in the places I have chosen.

24. I can be sure that if I need legal or medical help, my race will not work against me.

25. If my day, week, or year is going badly, I

need not consider whether each negative episode or situation whether it has racial overtones.

26. I can choose blemish cover or bandages in "flesh" color and have them more or less match my skin.[2]

~

DISCUSSION

Do you agree that the list amounts to privileges some people have over others? Why or why not?

Which of these privileges do you have? Does the amount of your privileges surprise you?

Peggy McIntosh says these privileges are often invisible. Why do you think that is? Why is it helpful to expose them?

What are ways you can use your privileges to empower others?

EXERCISE

Break into groups of four or five. Go around and take one minute to answer each of these questions.

Round One
What are one or more ways in which you've had unearned disadvantage in your life?

Round Two
What are one or more ways in which you've had unearned advantage in your life?

Round Three
How do you feel talking about and hearing these experiences of unearned advantage and disadvantage?

APPLICATIONS

FINAL REFLECTIONS

What was the most important thing you learned through this study?

What are some ways you can continue to learn and grow? What are books, documentaries, and websites that can help you grow in your knowledge of racial reconciliation?

What are some relationships that have changed as a result of the assignments. How can you continue to grow in having diverse groups of friends?

What questions do you still have about issues of racial reconciliation?

What are some practical applications for you, your church, and your community?

What does the Gospel mean for these issues?

How can loving and following Jesus change your heart, mind, and practices?

APPENDIX

LEADER'S NOTES

Praise God for your willingness to lead the church in this important discussion! You're starting on a journey to help bring reconciliation to the lives of the people around you, your community. I have a few notes and encouragements for you as you begin to plan for the class.

Before the Class

One critical aspect to having a fruitful class is to have a diverse group of people to participate in the class. One of the central ways people will learn during this class is by listening to the diverse viewpoints of those in the class. Here are a few things to think about.

Class Diversity

Ask minorities in your church if they would be willing to join the class. Tell them you think their viewpoint is important and will help the class learn.

Think about not only racial minorities in your church but also those from various socioeconomic backgrounds. Also think about a good mix of genders and age groups.

If you don't have much diversity in your church, consider asking some mature believers outside of your church.

Take sign-ups and think about the people who are signing up. Are there any missing demographics? Why do you think some groups are unwilling to participate?

Advertising the Class

Advertise the class to your congregation. If you are the pastor, consider preaching a sermon on racial reconciliation from the various texts presented in the curriculum. Ask the church whether they know how to process the various racial social tensions through the lens of the Bible.

Class Size

A small class size (5–10 people) can be an enormous blessing as long as there is some diversity and people who are willing to listen and learn from each other.

Consider capping the number of people who can signup for the class if you anticipate a large turnout. If the group is larger than twenty, there is a tendency for introverted people to never speak. The class can become a monologue instead of a genuine conversation between people in the class. When you cap the class, you can either have multiple classes simultaneously or wait to teach the class again during another season.

The other alternative is to divide the class into smaller groups during the discussion section. Consider recruiting another leader (as many as necessary) to lead these breakout discussion groups.

During the Class

As you set up for the class, consider having people face each other if the size is manageable. Otherwise wait for the discussion to seat in a circle for the breakout groups.

As the class begins, explain that there may be many issues where people will disagree with the material or with the opinion of other people in the class. Tell them it's ok to disagree with anything or anybody but we are all called to *"speak the truth in love"* (Eph. 4:15). Encourage people to use a tone that is respectful and full of grace even when we disagree with each other.

You may want to consider beginning the class with a video that fits the theme of the material for that class. Consider showing teaching from minority voices, especially if your class has few of them attending.

Don't let any of the participants dominate the discussion. Make sure you hear from a good variety of people in the class. Kindly tell the overenthusiastic that it's important to hear from everyone.

Proactively ask the opinions of those who have been silent in the class.

Finally encourage people to live out the study each week. At the end of every section there is a real-world application to the people in our lives. Explain to them the significance of acting upon those truths we have learned together. Before the start of every class, open the floor for stories of people who have boldly applied the lesson to people in their lives. Share from your own life, what God is doing through these studies. Feel free to also openly discuss your own failures to live out the lesson and in humility ask the participants to help you do better each week.

May God give you grace and encourage to effectively lead your people in a season of growth and healing.

NOTES

A Racially Divided Society

1. Michael Emerson, Christian Smith, *Divided by Faith: Evangelical Religion and the Problem of Race in America* (Oxford: Oxford University Press, 2001), 7.
2. Richard Rothstein, *The Color of Law: A Forgotten History of How our Government Segregated America* (New York: Liveright Publishing Corporation, 2018).
3. Amanda Petrusich, "Darius Rucker and the Perplexing Whiteness of Country Music," *The New Yorker*, October 25, 2017, http://www.www.newyorker.com/culture/cultural-comment/darius-rucker-and-the-perplexing-whiteness-of-country-music/
4. Michael Lipka, "Many U.S. Congregations Are Still Racially Segregated, but Things Are Changing," Pew Research Center, December 8, 2014, accessed March 17, 2017, http://www.pewresearch.org/fact-tank/2014/12/08/many-u-s-congregations-are-still-racially-segregated- but- things-are-changing-2/
5. Jeremy Tisby, *The Color of Compromise* (Grand Rapids: Zondervan, 2019), 38.
6. Emerson, 55.

Race and Racism

1. https://www.pcaac.org/racial-and-ethnic-reconciliation-study-committee-report/
2. Committee on Mission to North America. "Pastoral Letter on Racism." PCAHISTORY.org. http://www.pcahistory.org/pca/racism.pdf (accessed March 19th, 2019).
3. David Stevens, *God's New Humanity: A Biblical Theology of Multi-ethicity for the Church* (Eugene: Wipf & Stock, 2012), 103.
4. John Hope Franklin, *The Color Line* (Colombia: University of Missouri, 1993), 72–73.

Christ the Reconciler

1. Ken Sande, *The Peacemaker: A Biblical Guide to Resolving Personal Conflict* (Grand Rapids: Baker Books, 2007), 209.

The Multi-Ethnic Church

1. Stevens, *God's New Humanity*, 133.
2. Craig S. Keener, *Acts, An Exegetical Commentary Volume 2* (Grand Rapids: Baker Academic, 2012), pg. 1535
3. Ibid, 1560

Cultural Intelligence

1. National Public Radio, "Babies of Color Are Now the Majority", July 1, 2016, http://www.npr.org/sections/ed/2016/07/01/ 484325664/babies-of-color-are-now-the- majority-census-says.
2. David Jacobus Bosch, *Transforming Mission: Paradigm Shifts in Theology of Mission* (Maryknoll: Orbis Books, 2011), 466.
3. Soong-Chan Rah, *The Next Evangelicalism: Releasing the Church from Western Cultural Captivity* (Downers Grove, Ill: IVP, 2009), 9.
4. Rah, *The Next Evangelicalism*, 10.
5. Rah, *The Next Evangelicalism*, 11.

The Call to Justice

1. Timothy Keller, *Generous Justice: How God's Grace Makes Us Just* (New York: Dutton, Penguin, 2010), 3–4.
2. The U.S. Census Bureau, "Quarterly Residential Vacancies and Homeownership, Second Quarter 2017", July 27, 2017, https:// www.census.gov/housing/hvs/files/ currenthvspress.pdf.
3. Jemar Tisby, "Trayvon Martin's Death and a Resurgent Civil Rights Movement in America, January 26, 2017, https://www. raanetwork.org/fifth-anniversary- trayvon-martins-death/
4. Michelle Alexander, *The New Jim Crow* (New York: The New Press, 2010).
5. Timothy Keller, *Generous Justice: How God's Grace Makes Us Just* (New York: Penguin Books, 2016), 67–68.

Privilege and Grace

1. Doug Serven, *Heal Us, Emmanuel: A Call for Racial Reconciliation, Representation and Unity in the Church* (Oklahoma City: White Blackbird Books, 2016).
2. Peggy McIntosh, "White Privilege: Unpacking the Invisible Knapsack," *Peace and Freedom Magazine*, July/August 1989.

ABOUT WHITE BLACKBIRD
BOOKS

White blackbirds are extremely rare, but they are real. They are blackbirds that have turned white over the years as their feathers have come in and out over and over again. They are a redemptive picture of something you would never expect to see but that has slowly come into existence over time.

There is plenty of hurt and brokenness in the world. There is the hopelessness that comes in the midst of lost jobs, lost health, lost homes, lost marriages, lost children, lost parents, lost dreams, loss.

But there also are many white blackbirds. There are healed marriages, children who come home, friends who are reconciled. There are hurts healed, children fostered and adopted, communities restored. Some would call these events entirely natural, but really they are unexpected miracles.

The books in this series are not commentaries, nor are they meant to be the final word. Rather, they are a collage of biblical truth applied to current times and places. The authors share their poverty and trust the

Lord to use their words to strengthen and encourage his people. Consider these books as entries into the discussion.

May this series help you in your quest to know Christ as he is found in the Gospel through the Scriptures. May you look for and even expect the rare white blackbirds of God's redemption through Christ in your midst. May you be thankful when you look down and see your feathers have turned. May you also rejoice when you see that others have been unexpectedly transformed by Jesus.

Made in the USA
Monee, IL
14 November 2020